MW00529769

HOUSE 418

THE CIRCLE SQUARED

ISBN 978-1-914166-02-0 (Hardcover)
ISBN 978-1-914166-03-7 (Paperback)

A catalogue for this title is available from the British Library.
10 9 8 7 6 5 4 3 2 1

First published in 2021 by Hadean Press
West Yorkshire
England

WWW.HADEANPRESS.COM

HOUSE 418

THE CIRCLE SQUARED

Cath Thompson

For Jim

CONTENTS

Opening Remarks

The purpose of this book is to introduce the initiatory theory and practice that was developed over a forty-year period of research and experiment by the first and second generations of E. Qaballistic magicians.

An initiatory ritual reinforces what magical ability the candidate already possesses, and stabilises the personality within the context of the magical universe delineated by the particular system of ritual employed. These are usually based on a fourfold template symbolised by a cross or a quartered circle which represents the four Cardinal points, the four seasons of the solar year, the four phases of the lunar cycle, or any other of the many traditional quartets of magical forces, including the astrological Triplicities of Earth, Air, Fire, and Water. Astrology provides a celestial context which anchors ritual and operator in real observable space-time by the intentional correlation of events. E. Qaballistic ritual magic is astrologically synchronised on the principle that everything born of a moment in time is characterised by the forces influencing that moment. Planetary days and hours become more effective when the planet itself is well aspected, and stellar combinations open the esoterica of mythology to the possibility of specific ritualised allegory in a moment whose future is already defined.

Part One

1. THE SUN-VENUS

Sun conjunct Venus is one of the best aspects in natal astrology and so the calculation SUN + VENUS = 107 = MAGICIAN was immediately interesting from the beginning of EQ, suggesting a magician's configuration and a ritual of some importance. This idea was corroborated by the fact the Sun-Venus conjunctions form a pentagram over an eight-year period. The reference to the "five pointed star" in *Liber AL* I:60 added confirmation from within the context of the Holy Book itself.

The geometry of the shape holds a key to its magical significance, for the lines and intersections of the star contravene the early Pythagorean insistence on whole numbers by having a ratio of measurement which cannot be exactly represented, but expands decimally without ever stopping or coming to a repeating sequence. This is called an irrational number in mathematics. The Pythagorean philosopher credited with the discovery of irrational numbers in the 5th century BCE was Hippasus of Metapontum, who according to Iamblichus was drowned for his impiety, although he may only have been exiled. Be that as it may, his discovery made a lasting impact. Centuries later the great mathematician Kepler called it a precious jewel and one of the treasures of geometry. Each line of the pentagram is intersected at two places, and the subsections are in the ratio of 1:1.1618..., symbolised by the Greek letter Phi. It is the Golden Ratio or Golden Section, sometimes called the Divine Proportion, which is the basis of the well-known Fibonacci sequence. The five-pointed Star embodies the Golden Ratio and is thus primarily a symbol of harmonious evolutionary force. It was associated with health both physical and spiritual long before the Christian era.

The pentagram has continued to feature in European magical tradition, gathering all sorts of fivefold significances, and even being classified as either "good" or "evil" depending upon its angle of rotation. Several generations of occultists since the heyday of the "Magical Revival" have cut their ritualistic teeth with the Lesser Banishing Rite of the Pentagram, and it is still a popular and effective opening ceremony for cleansing and establishing the four Quarters. Repeated daily performance over a period of a few months will have some initiatory effect. The mathematical significance of the pentagram, and the constant redrawing of it in the heavens by the Sun and Venus, however, remain largely disconnected from most areas of occult study.

The Sun and Venus are the astro-magical Lord and Lady of the heavens. The Sun is the Life-giving God-King, and Venus is the Goddess of Love and Beauty, the Queen of Nature. Their conjunction is allegorised in the alchemical wedding, the union of the Cross and the Rose, and marked in time at each point of the celestial pentagram. The magical effect is a purification and a balancing of all the Elements with their opposites, which will occur by default once participation has begun with a ritual synchronised with the Sun-Venus conjunction closely applying.

The Sun-Venus is an initiatory configuration, and every ritual celebration has an effect, no matter whether Venus is retrograde or not. In 40 years I have known it to be performed by groups of occultists and by single practitioners, by heterosexual couples and homosexual couples, by Solar Priestesses and Priests of Venus, skyclad under the night-stars or in full ceremonial regalia and furnished Temple surroundings. The polarities of the Sun-Venus are not those of physically gendered human sexuality but of human spirituality.

The "Supreme Deity" of *Liber AL* is the Infinite Nothingness which contains Everything, and is addressed poetically as the Goddess, a continuous and omnipresent Negative that divides for love's sake to reunite and create Positive manifestation. The Goddess of Infinite Space has the ultimate power of rulership, thus the authority of the Sun-Venus is with Venus, as Her planet is the mundane Chakra of the Goddess of Love. The Sun-God of the Zodiac governs in Her Name. Honest sincerity of the ritualist is more important than sexual identity, for the polarity of Being and Not-being is the same for all would-be Magicians, and is not suitably juxtaposed with the masculine/feminine polarity of gender.

Although magic per se is not mysticism and does not concern itself with questions of religion or philosophy, it does present the beginner with a reality that is greater than the thinking intelligence alone can easily accommodate. The Sun-Venus Ritual in this book is a magician's initiation that balances the self-identifying consciousness with that which is identified as not-self. By ritually marking the moment of the Sun-Venus we are correlating ourselves with the first point of the pentagram as it is being drawn in the Solar system, and inviting that celestial refinery to function within our own magical sphere.

As for the timing of a Sun-Venus, a good aspect to the Moon helps with the reflecting of the stellar influence into the mundane; a good aspect to Jupiter brings some harmonious expansion; a conjunction with Fortuna will bestow additional purification. Mars adds energy but needs careful supervision. Mercury brings swift logic to the alchemical transmutation but may steal something of the original idea. Saturn brings impedance and heavy dullness and is not very helpful except in Libra. The outer planets are sometimes difficult to account for, everybody has got to be somewhere, and they are generally best ignored unless forming inimical configurations, in which case complete and immediate cancellation must be considered. This recommendation applies to Mars and Saturn as well. Once the decision has been taken to mark the moment in ritual, a connection in Time is made towards that future moment, and it will begin to affect the present. In effect, the ritual has begun.

The initiatory process of the Sun-Venus falls into four stages which run parallel to the so-called Magical Powers of the Sphinx: to Know, to Dare, to Will, and to keep Silent. We start out knowing what we are doing, and then we dare to wonder, to doubt, and to ask questions, whose answers may only be discovered if we have the will to endure until everything else is still and quiet. The first part is a taking-stock of the current situation and making judgements about it. The second part is a breakdown and disintegration of the first. The third part is a vague and wearisome toil; and the fourth is an awakening into a fresh coherence of integrated consciousness. Individual experiences vary of course, and so does the timescale, but the general pattern has remained consistently recognisable over forty years in a variety of circumstances among more than two dozen different occultists.

It is worth noting that KNOW + DARE + WILL = 107 = HOUSE OF GOD which in astrological terms is the 10th House. The cusp of the Tenth is the position of the Midheaven and the South Cardinal, and it is the House of Authority in a chart. It is ruled by Capricorn, and in the context of the Sun-Venus it is symbolic of the culmination of the initiatory experience: SILENCE = 107 = HOUSE OF GOD. Capricorn has a dualistic nature being an Earth Sign whose zodiac animal, the Goat, is renowned for its high climbing and agility, yet whose planetary ruler is the slow-moving Saturn. CAPRICORN = 121, the balance of the Two (Self and Not-self) between two singularities.

2. THE ORDEAL X

The whole sequential experience is known to E. Qaballists as the "Ordeal X", a phrase found in *Liber AL* III:22 that aptly describes the psychological stresses that ensue after celebrating a Sun-Venus conjunction. ORDEAL X = 75 = CUBE, the extension of the established four into the harmonic six in three dimensions, through the evolutionary force of the five-pointed pentagram. 75 is the value of BEAST, or Be As T where T = 24 = GOD.

Beginning with the immediate balance of the Sun-Venus Ritual symbolised by Libra, the candidate enters a "Hall of Judgement" (ORDEAL X = 75 =OSIRIS) which induces a re-assessment of 'what is and what is not,' or Self and Not-Self. This sometimes becomes a personal crisis of disintegration as the candidate progresses through the transformative breakdown represented by Scorpio, and the healing alchemy of Sagittarius. In Capricorn the candidate becomes the BALANCED ONE = 128 = THE ORDEAL X, SUN AND VENUS, BAPHOMET and SCARLET WOMAN.

These are the four Zodiac Signs of the Autumn months, busy with festivals and ceremonies for the harvest, and for the lighting of fires, and for the souls of the dead. They are synchronous with the

Solar journey from the Equinox at Libra, the Sign of Judgement, and through Death in Scorpio, metamorphosing through Sagittarius to rebirth on the Winter Solstice when the Sun enters Capricorn. It is a time for transmuting and transforming, for rectifying and refining the energies of the year that has passed.

The Zodiac describes a continuous cycle of life. The astrological year (using the Tropical rather than the Sidereal Zodiac) begins on the first day of Spring, the Vernal Equinox, when the Sun enters the Sign of Aries. Aries is placed in the first House as the Sign of birth, the Eastern horizon being where the new day begins. The twelve Zodiac signs tell their story about human life, starting here with the birth of the individual. In Taurus the baby takes possession of its own physical being and its immediate surroundings. The next sign is Gemini, the Sign and House of Communication, in which the child grows to adolescence: followed by the Fourth House, Cancer, representing the home. In this stage the individual becomes a fully-grown adult who is capable of maintaining their own space and environment. In the Solar year this is where Summer begins, the Sun entering Cancer at the Solstice. The next Sign, Leo, is the prime of life when goals have been achieved, ideally, and our hypothetical individual is king or queen of the castle. The year rolls on to Virgo, and harvest time, and the individual begins to reap what he or she has sown in their youth. This is the Sixth House, and it is associated with matters of health and sickness. And now we have come to the Autumn Equinox and the Seventh House which although it is the House of the partner, also represents the immediate opposition, whatever is facing the personality of the Ascendant. In this context it is the inescapable mortality of the individual, who is entering the Judgement Hall of Osiris, represented by the Libran Scales of Justice. This is the last stage of earthly life. Death, of course, happens in the full Autumn with the Sun in Scorpio, when Nature herself appears to be dying. Sagittarius, the Ninth House, ruler of long journeys and matters of religion and philosophy, represents the immediate post-mortem experience, as the life energies and vital forces are withdrawn from the body, and the discorporated individual becomes detached from the material world. This is a mysterious period of transition between states, well symbolised by the Centaur who is half-man, half-horse. When the refinement is complete the individual consciousness is reborn in the light of Capricorn. Then Aquarius the Water-Bearer carries the life-spark through the Eleventh House of hopes and wishes, and pours it into Pisces, Sign of the Fishes. And from here, in the concealment and secrecy of the Twelfth House, it is ready to be born again.

The magickally useful part of this cycle is in the four Zodiac signs of Autumn, Libra, Scorpio, Sagittarius and Capricorn, and the measurement of a period of time in which it is theoretically possible to negotiate with Death to create a desired change in the future.

Astrologers will note that within these four signs is the period known as the Via Combusta or Burning Way. This portion of the Zodiac lies between 15 degrees Libra and 15 degrees Scorpio, and is reckoned an unfortunate position, especially for the Moon. The Moon's influence extends through the rhythms of life, the ebb and flow of tides and of the menstrual cycle; She mediates the spiritual light of the Sun as a magical force characterised by the Sign She is in, and the magical effect of Scorpio is that of a full stop. It is the point in the cycle where evolution and chance meet, and the impossible becomes necessary. Blood haemorrages safely as the womb is renewed. The symbolism surrounding Scorpio is of great significance in English Qaballa.

A star map shows that within this area of the night sky is the constellation of Ophiucchus, between Scorpio and Sagittarius. The mythology and name of Ophiucchus is not as old as some of the other constellations; he has associations with Apollo and seems to have been holding a serpent before he became a healer. His position between the sign of Death and the Centaur – who is also a healer – is suggestive of a post-mortem ritual.

This portion of the Zodiac, Libra-Scorpio-Sagittarius-Capricorn, represents the process of the Judgement Hall of Osiris and the passage into the afterlife. It is the mechanism that ensures the continuity of life. From a mortal point of view it is disastrous, but from a mystical point of view it is triumphant, hence the expression in AL III:22, "the *winners* of the Ordeal X".

In EQ the value of the four Signs is 58+93+146+121 = 418. This accords with the description of "the name of thy house 418" as a "fourfold" mystery at the end of the second chapter of *Liber AL*. It also reiterates the idea of a process of change and resolution and refinement and regeneration, an initiatory formula in four parts.

3. FOUR HUNDRED & EIGHTEEN

The number 418 appears in *Liber Al vel Legis* Chapter I verse 46, "Nothing is a secret key of this law; Sixty-one the Jews call it; I call it eight, eighty, four hundred & eighteen", and in Chapter II verse 78, "They shall worship thy name, foursquare, mystic, wonderful, the number of the man, and the name of thy house 418."

On the face of it, at first glance as it were, the number is explained as being concomitant with the Hebrew G-D which has the value in that Kabbalah of 61, and which is presumably Kether. The key of the law is the Nothing which the Jews call "sixty-one" and which Liber AL calls "four hundred & eighteen." 418 is the Nothing from which Manifestation extends, and it is a numeric symbol of the abode referred to in the second quote. The prophet of *Liber AL* has a house named 418, which is the name *Liber AL* gives to the Jews' concept of Nothing; the house of the prophet is thus correlated with 61. This suggests a state or condition of God-like perfection, in which the prophet dwells.

This interpretation is more or less acceptable, if taken in isolation. But *Liber AL* is a Holy Book in English, and its gematria is by its own "order & value of the English Alphabet." One does not translate a Holy Book into another language to analyse its contents once one has obtained the correct enumeration of the original writing. *Liber AL* I:46-7 goes on with "but they have the half," which suggests that the Hebrew Tree is not the whole story as far as the *Book of the Law* is concerned. This proposition was proved in some of the earliest E. Qaballistic investigation of the text, with the delineation of the Complete Tree of Life in the 28 characters of *Liber AL* II:76. Our study of 418 cannot exclude other E. Qaballistic conclusions.

4. 418 IN *LIBER AL VEL LEGIS*

English Qaballistic analysis often starts with the examination of context within *Liber AL*, the simple meaning of the phrase, and how the words, numbers, or letters are used. A closer look often reveals the same numerical value repeated more than once in a verse or across a sequence of verses. It is interesting to note that in the second quote given above, the words WORSHIP + FOURSQUARE + MYSTIC + WONDERFUL = 418. The reiteration of the number within the same sentence emphasises its significance with some suggestions as to its nature. The Key of the Law is a "foursquare" mystery of worship and wonder rather than a Trinity as we might have supposed from *AL* I:46's three-part "8, 80, 418". The "house" named 418 is more than a Gentile version of the Hebrew Kabbalist's G-D. We must broaden our research and look for the number elsewhere in *Liber AL* for more clues as to its significance.

418 is the value of *AL* Ch II:75, "Aye! listen to the numbers & the words," a command immediately followed by "4 6 3 8 A B K 2 4 A L G M O R 3 Y X 24 89 R P S T O V A L," the 28 symbols which are the unfolding of the Complete Tree of Life revealed in *AL* II:76. The instruction to pay attention to the sounds of the numbers and words is symbolic of

418, the Key of the Law. This adds some weight to the idea that the number has something to do with the Nothing from which Everything extends. 418 has prepared the prophet's intellect to receive the revelation of II:76, and remains in the text as a guide for all to read.

The phrase "unveiling of the Company of Heaven" (*AL* I:2) adds to 418 and it seems reasonable to suppose that the phrase might pertain to actions involved at the beginning of something, especially since this is only the second verse of the *Book of the Law*. We may expand this idea of unveiling to a description of the act of Creation itself, since the Creation is implied in the reference to the sounds of words and numbers already associated with 418. In EQ the value of WORD is 28 which is the number of spheres on the Complete Tree, making the composite symbol a Word in itself, a simple and clear correspondence with traditions of the Word from AUM to LOGOS which we need explore no further at the moment.

AL I:50 "A word to say about the Hierophantic task" has the value 418 and is another piece of evidence in favour of the idea that 418 is connected with the sounds of words that cause manifestation to occur. Here we must acknowledge the established scientific laws concerning the physics of matter and quantum theory, remembering that "sub-atomic" appears in the text of *Liber AL*, but we will keep to our theme. The similarities between the creation poetry of the scientist and of the qaballist are a diversion for another time.

To recap, our study of the number 418 has so far shown that it symbolises a precursor to manifestation, a pre-creation condition which is similar to the Hebrew Negativity beyond Kether. Since this is stated in *AL* I:46, where "Nothing" is called 418, we have merely unpicked the declaration. We have not quite explained how 418 comes to be the "name of thy house" and as yet we have not approached the meaning of "thy house", for there is another phrase in *Liber AL* that adds to 418 which must be introduced to our collection. It is verse 36 of Chapter 3, "Then said the prophet unto the God." Again there is the reference to the spoken word, but what follows is a very particular initiatory ritual, which seems to be moving the focus away from the familiar and traditional areas of creation mythology that we have touched upon so far.

Immediately before this appearance of 418, *AL* III:35 says "The half of the word of Heru-ra-ha, called Hoor-pa-kraat and Ra-Hoor-Khut," one of the verses in *Liber AL* that seems out of place and disconnected from the sequence of the text. We may deduce that the "half of the word" is that which is referred to in Chapter One as mentioned above, "the Jews...have the half." RA HOOR KHUT=NOTHING and HOOR PA KRAAT=SECRET support this proposition as "Nothing is a secret key of this Law." The thirty-fifth verse of the third chapter is reminding us of the nature of the number which is to be expressed in the next verse: "Then Said The Prophet Unto The God" which has the total value 418. This is followed by a poetic translation of the hieroglyphs upon the Stele of Revealing, an invocation spoken by Ankh-af-na-Khonsu. Here it is worth noting the initial letters of those seven words TSTPUTG = 131 = EXORCIST, and the final letters NDETOEG = 107 = MAGICIAN; the E. Qaballistic technique of finding the first essence of meaning at the beginning of a phrase and its final transmutation at the end reveals the offices of the Priest upon the Stele.

418 is once again a precursor at the introduction of the Ritual, and towards the end of *AL* III:38 we find the house motif appears again: "Bid me within thine House to dwell, O winged snake of light, Hadit!" We may surmise from the context that this is the "house" named 418, and to dwell therein is a situation or condition that may be achieved as a magical result of correctly performing the Ritual.

The reminder in *AL* III:35 of the half that the Jews have, and at the end of *AL* III:37 the expression "thine house" are two threads that continue from our first examination. The connection with the Complete Tree of Life remains apparent, albeit somewhat blurred, unless that is the core meaning of 418. We know that 418 is Nothing, however, and there must be more than metaphysical mind-bending in our proposed interpretation.

We seem to have got as far as we can go with the text of *Liber AL* and the reference it gives us to the Hebrew system. There can be no doubt that there is more to the number 418. Indeed, if it is similar to AIN it must be a major component in the system of English Qaballa, for it is the E. Qaballistic view that primary archetypal ideas remain the same across all ages and civilisations, by the simple reason that they derive from observations of natural phenomena and human physiology. The idea of Nothing preceding Something is not exclusive to the Kabballists, in fact most Creation myths begin with an archetype of negativity, the space in the Womb of the Mother. The E. Qaballistic creation describes the negativity dividing into two negative states which unite to form a positive condition (*AL* I:28-30), but 418 seems to be a more precisely defined phenomena than these abstractions. We must extend our search parameters beyond the text of *Liber AL* and look for 418 in other places, leaving the complexities of pre-creation existence on one side for the moment. The correspondences with the Hebrew system as delineated in the "Western Occult Revival" can only go as far as the 22 letters permit; they are comprehensive but incomplete and even contradictory, and moreover lacking in consistency with modern technological developments. The modern magician is starting with a different mindset from that of his ancient forbears, although the phenomena he engages with are changeless from one era to another. The latter statement must be correct, else there would be no modern magicians. We must find another system of correspondences and make a fresh start, taking our number, 418, away from *Liber AL* and away from the Kabbalist references: armed only with the English Qaballistic Alphabet, we shall look for evidence pertaining to 418 in a different place.

5. 418 IN ASTROLOGY

The Hebrew Kabbalah is not very ancient, in the scheme of things. Estimates vary, but the archaeological picture of the Middle East suggests that the written language is perhaps four thousand years old. A much older set of archetypes is to be found in the astrological canon.

418 is the value of LIBRA + SCORPIO + SAGITTARIUS + CAPRICORN, the Judgement Hall of Osiris in the Zodiac, as discussed above. As a formula of that which precedes manifestation, which was our first notion of 418, it is undoubtedly interesting. As an opening statement for an initiation ritual, it is effective. As the "name of thy house" it indicates a dynamic environment. Our analysis of 418 holds itself together adequately so far.

Looking at the Complete Tree of Life indicated by *AL* II:76 we find that the value of the first ten characters of the verse, (the branches of the Tree), 4+6+3+8+A(=1)+B(=20)+K(=9)+2+4+A(=1), is the value of LIBRA, 58; the value of the next eight characters (the trunk of the Tree) is 93 = SCORPIO. The last ten characters (the roots of the Tree) have the same value as MANIFESTATION. The symbols of Judgement and Death are rehearsed in the perfected Tree (Libra) and the connection (Scorpio) with Manifestation at the roots. Libra is the Balance of Heaven, a dimension of dynamic equilibrium; Scorpio is the means of communication between Heaven and Earth, dividing and uniting the two conditions. Libra-Scorpio is a complex within 418 as well as part of the sequence, as suggested by the presence of the Burning Way across the cusp of the two Signs, and their sum total 58+93=151 = EIGHTEEN, and CERTAINTY. Certainty is a state of comprehending knowledge which is beyond doubt, which cannot be questioned or degraded.

It is worth noting here that the word 'eighteen' has the highest of all the letter-values that are mentioned by name in *Liber AL* rather than written as digits. It is the value of the letter F which is attributed to GEMINI = THE LIGHT and BREATHED: We all are born, live in the medium of Time, and die; and there is a dimension of consciousness which is continuous, an Eternity in which we exist forever, but rarely glimpse.

A study of the characteristics of each Sign should clarify the four stages of our proposed "Nothing which precedes Creation" and reveal the Key of the Law in more detail.

6. 418 IN SYMBOLS

The Scales of LIBRA=58 are the one inanimate emblem in the Zodiac. They are the Scales of Justice or Absolute Measurement. In the Egyptian myth the Scales weigh the heart of the deceased against the Feather of Maat, which means "Truth". Only the weightlessness of one pure enough to walk on water would pass the test, otherwise the Scales must tip and Time will go on.

58 is the value of HOUSE, meaning that the number is the Abode of Harmonious Justice. If Perfect Balance were achieved there would be nothing else, no other existence or non-existence. Libra is the quantum wave of all probabilities balanced at the moment of collapse; the observation of the weight in the scale pan causes the event. It is the eternal idea of a position, or point in space which is always bound to move in Time making every conscious Now moment a new definition from a different location.

LIBRA = 58 = HADIT. Hadit is the infinitely tiny particle. Light is the means by which we observe particles, and anything smaller than a particle or wave of light remains invisible. Hadit is hidden by light. *Liber AL* II:1 says "Nu! the hiding of Hadit," where the shapes of the letters *nu* join to make a waveform; to round off the correspondences with the vocabulary used in particle physics, the smallest particle is called a QUARK = 58 = HADIT.

58 is the value of the first section of *AL* II:76, "4 6 3 8 A B K 2 4 A". The ten characters are arranged after the pattern of the Perfect Tree of the Hebrew tradition. In the English Qaballa it represents a dimensional environment or condition which is not necessarily simply "transcendent", but having additional characteristics more in common with sub-atomic theory, is nonetheless an effective symbol of what is often called "Heaven". The infinitely tiny particle, Hadit, the disturbance in space that is hidden by Nu, is the event of the division of Nothing, for love's sake.

Number is the primary symbol in E. Qaballistic analysis. Ideas suggested by correspondence of numeric value tend to cluster around the main symbol like a swarm of bees around the queen, or like crystals growing out of a saturated solution, lending coherence and intelligibility to an otherwise fluid and abstract concept. The number is thus viewed from different places, as it were, and has its own story-pattern. Often this will link one number with another. 418 is a process, and 58 is how it begins, in a state of dynamic balance, a moment in which all possibilities are coalesced in potential. The collapse is 93, and 93 is that which restores the equilibrium.

93 is the value of SCORPIO, the Zodiac Sign that follows Libra. 93 is the value of DIVIDE, and UNITY, and the eight characters in *AL* II:76 that

form the Trunk of the Complete Tree. 93 is the bridge between the Unmanifest and the Manifest, uniting and at the same time dividing the two states.

Scorpio is of course the Sign and House of Death; the disturbance of the Balance is death to the balance. The Balance exists beyond the boundaries of Time; the tipping of the Balance is also the beginning of Time, in any sense, as the infinite stillness of Nothing encounters itself. 93 is the value of TIME, and NATURE, and thus 93 is the matrix of existence.

93 is the value of BEING and ENDING, and also the value of BEGIN; it is how the impossible becomes necessary, and the unexpected becomes inevitable. 93 is both "Unity by Denial" and "Division by Affirmation". The mysteries of 93 defy rational logic and expand the imagination. 93 is the value of MOTHER and VIRGIN, and thus 93 remains untouchable and unstained by the infinity of its endless working, and attempting negotiations there is a perilous business.

93 is Death, following the Confession and Judgement in Libra, when the individual is stripped down to the soul. In the Solar year (Northern hemisphere) this is full Autumn with the Sun in Scorpio, and the season for remembering the dead; in the lunar menstrual cycle Scorpio is the time of bleeding when the lining of the womb is discarded. The central mystery is that life continues on through the apparent catastrophic end. Renewed

by the debris of autumn the earth will eventually be ready to germinate seeds again. This is the CERTAINTY = 151 that is LIBRA + SCORPIO = 151. In the Complete Tree symbol, Manifestation is sustained and expressed by Certainty, and Certainty is supported and maintained by Manifestation.

The third part of 418 is symbolised by Sagittarius, which is Latin for "Archer". The constellation seems always to have been seen as part man, part beast, and aiming an arrow at the red star Antares in the constellation of Scorpio. The associations with Chiron the wise healer are more recent, and many more strands of symbolism have been added through Tarot attributions, and through astrological understanding. Our E. Qaballistic analysis of 418 suggests that Sagittarius represents a stage of existence after death (SAGITTARIUS = 146 = HEREAFTER), a proposition which casts some light across the assortment of ideas presented by the Zodiac Sign and constellation.

Sagittarius is the Ninth House, ruling matters of philosophy and religion, and long journeys – attributions that are in accord with after-death experiences. The Arrow may be seen as a symbol of the soul, whether in flight or still notched to the bow string, the important detail being that although the Arrow is aimed it has not yet reached its destination. In the context of the 22 Paths on the Hebrew Tree, Sagittarius is between Yesod and Tiphareth, between the Mind-Mirror of Illusion and the Radiant Harmony of Everything, and again rehearses the concept of change from one state to another. Sagittarius is neither completely bestial, nor perfectly human, but somewhere in between, like a metamorphosis in freeze-frame. The Tarot card attributed to this Path is the Art card, and traditionally bears a portrayal of an alchemical union between opposites. Once more the theme is transition, or a means of transformation. There is also an unknowable quality here, for the alchemy is explained with allegory and metaphor rather than clear speech.

146 is the value of CONCUBINE, a woman who lives with a man as a wife but without the status of a wife. She has sexual relations with the man without being a harlot. Her position and rank, together with her EQ value, put her in this Sagittarian category of almost borderline symbols, distinctly individual and yet in between one social class of being and another.

The Sagittarius part of the 418 process is arduous and difficult. It is the dark end of the year, and the future (without technological comforts) is uncertain as the environmental conditions impinge upon survival. Some creatures hibernate until spring, living mysteriously through the cold and frost. In the Easter story, this interval corresponds with the three days when the body lay in the tomb, concealed by the stone. Whereas the actions of Libra and Scorpio are relatively easy to determine, Sagittarius is a period of mysterious and secret workings of dissolution and refinement, and a severe test of commitment on the part of the operator.

The greatest darkness is before the dawn after the longest night, when the Sun at last turns back towards the northern hemisphere. In the Tropical Zodiac this is the cusp of Capricorn, the final stage of 418. The Winter Solstice is the festival of rebirth. Whether it is measured by stone markers casting their slow-moving shadows on the ground, or by binary electronics casting pixelated numbers on a screen, the annual event is a fact of human life on this planet, celebrated or marked in some fashion by innumerable people and cultures, continuously, from the unremembered past to the present day.

Astrologically, Capricorn rules the 10th House which signifies the authority in the chart, the reigning power, and so forth. In late December the God-Child is born and the Sun rises to begin regaining its strength and power. The date is not constant, but in the context of the English Qaballa the preferred day for celebration is the 21st.

The constellation of Capricorn is the smallest of all the Zodiac and has been represented as a goat, or a goat with the tail of a fish, since Babylonian times – even though its stars are faint it has always been associated with gods of power and wisdom. The Sign of the Goat has been associated with the Biblical Devil in the traditional Tarot, which seems a misinterpretation given the preceding comments about the festive season, and with the more modern concept of Baphomet in whom all the Elements are balanced, which is nearer the mark by EQ standards.

Our study has progressed with the addition of astrological principles. Extending our analysis of 418 to include the symbolism of the Zodiac has clarified and expanded the correspondence of the number. We began with *Liber AL*'s reference to Nothing, "sixty-one, the Jews call it" as being a secret Key of the Law, which is called 418. We followed the number through the text of *Liber AL* and found it described as "foursquare, mystic, wonderful...the name of thy house." We proposed that 418 symbolises a state preceding the Creation, or a preparation for manifestation, and found evidence to support this in the introductory expressions AYE LISTEN TO THE NUMBERS & THE WORDS = 418 and THEN SAID THE PROPHET UNTO THE GOD = 418. We also have the concept of the sounds of words, the frequency vibrations that disturbed the original Nothing. Now we have obtained a closer view of 418 as a sequential process with four distinct stages, within the pattern of the Zodiac, which is the Circle of Life itself, having no beginning and no end. In this context, 418 contains within itself the secret of rebirth.

7. 418 AND THE ORDEAL X

The correspondences of the EQ Tarot with 418 are worth mentioning here. Assigned to Scorpio, Sagittarius, and Capricorn, are the letters ALW, which of course spell the word LAW. 93+146+121=360 which is the number of degrees in a circle, indicating a coherent juxtaposition of these three at the beginning of the alphabet. Libra is the 22nd letter, X. This suggests that between Libra at the 22nd alphabetical position and Scorpio at the first position there are 23=I, 24=T, 25=E, and 26=P, attributed to Fire, Earth, Water, and Air (remember that this is a cyclic sequence rather than linear), so that the four Elements bridge the gap between Justice and Death. After the end of 418 in Capricorn comes the rest of the Zodiac and planets with the remaining alphabetical letters.

418 is a story, like a Mystery Play, and it is about what goes on before the event of Creation, what must occur before the Light can exist, or be born again. It is a confirmation of the continuity of existence, even though the join from one cycle to the next cannot be seen. It is a pattern, a recipe, a formula, and a template. In the context of the ritual on the Stele of Revealing, in the final stanza, Hadit equates with Libra, Ra Hoor Khuit with Scorpio, Nuit with Sagittarius, and Ankh-af-na-Khonsu with

Capricorn. The Priest has identified both himself and the God whose power he has invoked, and has prepared himself to die. The secret door having been opened and with the star-splendour of Nuit above, the Self-Slain Priest dwells in the House of Hadit, and Ra Hoor Khuit abides there also.

A different sacrificial myth cycle is the Christian death and resurrection of Jesus Christ. Here the four episodes are fairly easy to determine. The judgement before Pontius Pilate happens in Libra, the Crucifixion is the Scorpio Death, the three days in the Tomb are the mysterious transformations of Sagittarius, and the Resurrection and Ascension to the Light of Heaven happens in Capricorn; these are the four stages of the Easter story. The festival of Easter occurs at the first full Moon after the Spring Equinox, and since the Sun at that season is in either Aries or Taurus, the full Moon being opposite must be in Libra or Scorpio.

All sorts of human endeavours can be interpreted according to the astrological correspondences of 418. A typical pilgrimage, for instance, begins with the judging of plans and preparations for the journey. After some part of the journey has been completed there comes an unexpected setback or an event which alters the traveller's ethos, perhaps enforcing a delay and a reassessment of earlier assumptions. The continuation of the journey then becomes more arduous to endure, and the end may seem less certain, until the goal finally appears in the distance.

8. 418 IN THEORY

What we have discussed so far was formulated by the first English Qaballists in the early years of working with *Liber AL*, and explored further over the next four decades. Bringing these ideas of 418 into the realm of the Zodiac and the progress of the Sun and Moon connected the numeric symbol with a matrix of time-based phenomena which the group could observe, predict, and ritualise. The next question was, what sort of ritual, for what sort of outcome? The discovery and proving of a new initiatory system which would be effective for all candidates was the longer aim of this research.

The Sun-Venus was the first practical demonstration of stellar initiation derived from the English Qaballa, and the basis for the first series of experiments with the 418 formula.

A lot of work was done with the number 93 and the Scorpio part of 418, most especially when the moon was traversing this quaternary. Lunar synchronicity was an obvious choice, the characteristics of the luminary's associated deities being familiar, and the frequency of the cycle enabling the performance of a series of repeated operations in a few months. An initiatory effect seemed a likely result. It became apparent that 93 was the catalysing part of the Ordeal X formula and that the dawning illumination of Capricorn revealed the purified substance.

For a time a different line of enquiry prevailed, beginning with EQ interpretations of "thy House". We had noted the idea of "House" already: HOUSE = 58 = ZODIAC so taking "thy House" as "thy Zodiac" and with Capricorn as the Tenth House being the Lord of the Zodiac, the general context of the next part of the exploration was fairly clear. The power of Libra Scorpio Sagittarius is crystallised in Capricorn, the House of the JUDGE = 75 = ORDEAL X. The "Ordeal X" seemed therefore to be something more than a generic title for all ordeals given by *Liber AL*.

The theory of 418 seemed sound enough, and the focus moved to the transformation and initiatory experience itself, and the question of what kind of a result might be expected by the candidate – which should be foreshadowed in some fashion by the final symbol, Capricorn. A similarity between the last and the first is not without precedent, indeed by EQ FIRST = FOURTH. The proposal that 418 is more than the template of the Ordeal X experience led to a second experiment which began in 2008 and continued for ten years.

9. 418 IN CONTEXT

Jim Lees wrote that "a course of action begins in Libra when one defines one's commitment to the project and thus disturbs the equilibrium of inactivity. In Scorpio comes the unexpected obstacles, when the original plan has to be modified to accommodate the unfolding circumstances. The Sagittarius phase is one of incoherence as the changes demanded by Scorpio are assimilated into the progress of the work, and in Capricorn the methods are perfected and the completion of the task is achieved." We had refined our understanding of the Zodiacal 418 to a more precise representation of the course of human activity than the old IAO formula. The next step was to ritualise these four stages.

We began with an 11-day solo practice comprising a Confessional, a Contemplation of Death, an Observation of the Post-Mortem, and a Meditation upon the Initiation. This was synchronised with the period of the Moon's transit through the four Signs, with the awareness of the lunar position relative to 418 held in our conscious minds throughout the period as a background condition which we could bring forward to more active contemplation when the opportunity arose. Many months of experiment ensued. Finally a ritual script was composed and made ready for others.

In the following year (2010) we undertook the first structured experimental ritual working aligned with 418, a programme which provided substantially similar results from seven magicians with different practical ritual experience, magical training, sexual preference, age, and social background. Our researchers all recorded similar feelings and fears. Alterations of mindset, dreamscapes, magical ambitions, and other attitudes were also consistent not only within the group but with the initiatory hypothesis, which itself was being proved and strengthened. Over the next few years the repeated performances continued, and the rituals were slightly edited by joint agreement.

The complete set of meditations and rituals are included below.

SOME CORRESPONDENCES OF 418

SUBJECT	LIBRA	SCORPIO	SAGITTARIUS	CAPRICORN
THEORY	JUDGEMENT	DEATH	TRANSITION	REGENERATION
SUNconjunctVENUS	CANDIDATE	DISINTEGRATION	RECTIFICATION	INITIATION
CARDINAL	EAST	NORTH	WEST	SOUTH
EVOLUTION	STASIS	CONVERSION	CONSOLIDATION	NEW VARIETY
EXISTENCE	LIFE	DEATH	REST	REBIRTH
PRINCIPLE	LOCATION	TIME	NOW	LIFE
SEPHIRAH	MALKUTH	BINAH	YESOD	NETZACH

Part Two

1. THE SUN-VENUS or 107 RITUAL

The Sun-Venus should be performed at least once before the 418 is attempted. The primary requirements are a Cup, and a quantity of port or claret; a beeswax candle; a wooden spill; and incense (rose, frankincense, benzoin, oudh, cedar, musk, sandalwood are all suitable).

THE SUN-VENUS or 107 RITUAL

To be performed in the hour of sunrise
with the Sun conjunct Venus applying
within
3 degrees.

PREPARATION

Perform your accustomed Temple opening and
purification. Then face the East, hands at chest level
with palms together, and say

In the Name of Life and the Infinite Law of Change

bringing the hands up to the forehead

*For the Honour of the Mother who unites and divides
all things*

bringing the unseparated hands straight down to
solar plexus level and then back up to chest level

In the Presence of the Eternal ever-coming Now

parting the hands

Here!

clapping the hands together

*This Holy Place is made ready to celebrate the union of the
Lady Venus with Her Lord the Sun. It is the hour of the
Dawn and the rising of the blissful ones in the vault of the
snake! They are a starlight kiss that regenerates the world!
Unity uttermost showed! I adore the Might of Thy Breath!
Thy Breath is the Core of every Star! The Flame of the
Breath of Life is Thy Name!*

light a beeswax candle and hold it up to the East

May Thy Eternal Fire bless this candle flame!

place the candle on the Altar.

*I call Raphael, Archangel of the East, appointed Guardian
of the Spirits of the Air!*

light incense

*Accept this perfume into Thy Element in all the quarters!
Let the sacrifice have no blood therein, and the worship of
the Lovely Star be a grace and a blessing upon the earth and
under the earth, on dry land and in the water, in the whirling
air and in the rushing fire!*

face South

*O Thou Continuous One of Heaven! To Thee in thy
watchtower of the south I burn the perfumes and draw thy
Star-shape!*

draw invoking pentagram of fire using the incense.

face West

*O Thou Continuous One of Heaven! To Thee in thy
watchtower of the West I burn the perfumes and draw thy
Star-shape!*

draw invoking pentagram of water using the
incense.

face North

*O Thou Continuous One of Heaven! To Thee in thy
watchtower of the North I burn the perfumes and draw thy
Star-shape!*

draw invoking pentagram of earth using the incense.
face East

O Thou Continuous One of Heaven! To Thee in thy watchtower of the East I burn the perfumes and draw thy Star-shape!

draw invoking pentagram of air using the incense.

O Thou Continuous One of Heaven! May thy incense sanctify this Cup

draw invoking pentagram of Spirit over the Cup using the incense.

May thy incense rise upon the wings of the morning to the gemmed azure of the firmament!

put the incense in its place.

Sweet wine, be thou blessed in the perfumed Chalice for the marriage feast and for beauty's sake be thou blessed!

pour wine into Cup

INVOCATION

face east, as the Sun rises with Venus

Thee I invoke, the Pentagram
Thee I invoke, the five-pointed Star of Silence
Thee I invoke, the Sign of the Magician
Thou art Scorpion
Thou art Sky-fire and Star-water
Thou art the Blue and the Red
Thine is the Royal Space!
Thou didst produce the Vault and the Snake – Thine is the
Ritual Word!
Thou didst produce the Golden Rule – Thine is the Pale
Sign!
Thou didst make the fourfold fifth
Thou didst make the Metal and the alloy
Thou didst create men to be divided and to be united
The Heart girt with a Pentagram is Thy Name.

ATTAINMENT

take flame from the beeswax candle with a
wooden spill

*Hear me, Five-pointed Star! and sanctify this Grail with
Thy spark!*

plunging the flame into the wine

*May this Cup be a starlight chalice at the wedding of the
Lady of Heaven and Her Lord!*

FEAST

raising the Cup to the East
There is no part of me that is not of the Stars!
I drink to the Company of Heaven, and the chance of union.
Do what thou wilt shall be the whole of the Law

drink

Love is the Law, Love under Will.

set the empty cup down

Let the rituals be performed with joy and beauty!
Amen.

Perform your accustomed closing ceremonies.

2. 418 IN PRACTICE (I)

The 418 takes nine successive months, beginning with the first full moon after the Spring Equinox and ending at the Winter Solstice. The start-date is more often Moon-Libra than Moon-Scorpio, and is an alignment used by several major world religions. In the first three months the entrance and passage of the Moon through the four Signs is noted, and time is set aside for meditating on the symbolism of each Sign. The operator takes note of the emotional and mental state, observing mood changes, and dreams, and also the sorts of events that seem to be synchronously portentous (such as seeing a particular animal or bird or coming across a familiar symbol in an unexpected setting) that make one feel that some other communication is occurring. This is a gentle exercise, the operator maintaining a background awareness of the lunar position to a reasonable degree of accuracy for the duration of the Lunar 418, which is roughly eleven days.

The Lunar 418 meditations or contemplations are relatively intuitive and flexible. Periods of time may be set aside for a structured meditation, or an Astral Temple may be maintained in the background of one's mind. It is important to get the timings correct. The lunar position is noted at 15 degrees

Libra in the first instance. The cusp of Libra-Scorpio, and 15 degrees Scorpio, are both marked in the second. The cusps of Sagittarius and Capricorn do not require such accurately synchronised observation, and a lunar position between 3 and 15 degrees is sufficient for the purpose.

In the second month, the operator may begin to identify his own being in linear time with the Moon's passage through the Signs. In Libra he should assess or judge himself, calmly and honestly: all is quite private. He should imagine his own death as an uncomplicated exit, and watch his own funeral with detachment. It is important to avoid mental and emotional unpleasantness in these exercises. The operator should wander easily along, rather than take the journey as a bare-knuckle ride. The meditation periods should be between 15 minutes and an hour, and the awareness of the Moon's progress maintained as before. In the Sagittarius and Capricorn phases the meditation should incorporate the observations and analyses of mood-changes, if any occur synchronistically with the change of Sign, as a focus.

In the third month, the meditations should become more focused. The judgement and sentence may be delivered by another. There may be a formal Confession. There may be a condemned cell. After the funeral, the graveside may be left untended and forgotten. Details of the story are filled in according to the operator's discretion. Again, it is important to avoid upsetting oneself; the details of mortality and the method of departure are irrelevant and the evocation of horror is pointless.

The Libra Meditation is about Confession. We place ourselves in the Judgement Hall, where there may be a Sword and Scales, or an Altar between two pillars, or similar appropriate symbols; the predominant colour is a pale green radiance, and the predominant atmosphere is of Inevitability. The examination of oneself is objective and unemotional. One is alone and can therefore be scrupulously honest without indulging in self-serving pity or glorification.

The Libra-Scorpio cusp Meditation is about the Dying Time. The sentence has been passed, and Death has come over the threshold. There may be a skull, or a fresh grave, or a deathbed. It is the cut-off point between past and future. The colours tend to be black and deep red, or the iridescent tones of beetle-wings and the pallor of decay, and the atmosphere is deadness, a stasis without characteristics. Nightmarish visualisations tend to be self-indulgences that are best avoided in this total acceptance. The pressure is released as the Moon crosses the 15th degree of Scorpio.

The Sagittarius Meditation is about what happens immediately after death. One waits, as if dead, for there is nothing else to be done. The funeral is over and the mourners have gone; the gravesite is perhaps no longer visited. It is an observation of one's inner Self (ego, imagination, reasoning mind, emotional faculty, and essential individual magical self) in the context of the lunar movement through the Sign. One does not impose any direction upon one's Will, for there is no knowing what may happen when we have departed from our mortality; marking the time and noting one's reactive responses is sufficient. One may experience synchronous dreams, and occurrences in the waking or Outer world which seem personally significant. The colours tend to be misty opalescences. The atmosphere is variable, sensed across a spectrum ranging from a heavy burdensome toil to a gentle caressing glimpse of joy.

The Capricorn Meditation is the fulfilment of the whole process, and is even more of a personal experience than that of the Sagittarius phase. Again there is no particular act of deliberate magical Will involved beyond the conscious marking of the Moon's passage into the Sign. It is a different mystery from the transitional period of Sagittarius, for it is the completion of the journey and the rebirth of the traveller. There may be any ambient colour and the atmosphere usually has some sense of culmination, and achievement.

3. 418 IN PRACTICE (II)

This sequence of Meditations is to be performed for three consecutive Lunar 418 periods, which will bring the course of the year to the Midsummer Solstice. This part of the Initiation must be properly carried out. It will attune the waking consciousness to the passage of the Moon through the Zodiac. It will prepare the individual for the more intimate experiences of the ritualised observations, which will have a greater initiatory impact than the Meditations because of the active involvement of the Magical Will in physical action and spoken word.

The Lunar 418 Rituals require a greater level of commitment than the Meditations. They are structured in such a way as to embody and enact the Meditation experience and follow the process through into the material world, matching up the waking mind's perception of the observable Outer world with the Inner. The Lunar 418 occupies approximately eleven days every month from start to finish, although the most intense portion lasts about three and a half days as the Moon traverses the Burning Way from 15 degrees Libra to 15 degrees Scorpio. The Rituals are timed to synchronise with the Moon's progress, and are to be performed for the next three months, between the Solstice and the Autumn Equinox.

A dedicated temple space with all the usual paraphernalia is not essential; the four Elemental Weapons, incense, pen and paper, and a candle, are the basic requirements.

1. Moon 15 Libra

To be performed when the Moon is at 15 degrees of Libra or as soon as possible thereafter.

Face East, feet together and arms outstretched (Sign of Osiris Slain), and say

In the Name of Life and Change, Whose Numbers and Words are 4, 6, 3, 8, A, B, K, 2, 4, A! In the Name of the Mother Virgin who is Time and who unites and divides Heaaven and Earth! Whose Numbers and Words are L, G, M, O, R, 3, Y, X! In the Name of the Eternal Ever-unfolding Now, Whose Numbers and Words are 24, 89, R, P, S, T, O, V, A, L!
I follow the Moon in the Burning Way across the Threshold of the Judge. I offer this incense in sacrifice - blessed be thou, creature of Earth and Fire: be thou a grateful perfume that is acceptable to the Time.

Light incense (Jasmine)

I invoke the Presence of Heru in the Scale of Justice!
May the Balance of Hadit hear my Confession!
I have turned away from the Love of God which is God.
My ideals are meaningless and my principles are mere vanity. I have neglected my plans, my courage has failed me, I am disharmonious and selfish and cruel: I am weak and dishonest: I have lived an illusion: my complacent inertia is

my downfall.
This is my judgement of myself.

Leave your Confession written on a piece of paper
on the Altar.

(Note: the Confession included is a working example.)

2. Moon Libra-Scorpio

To be performed as the Moon passes from
Libra to Scorpio.

At the end of Moon in Libra, face East, feet
together and arms outstretched (Sign of Osiris
Slain), and say

Bid me within thine house to dwell, o winged snake of light!

Light candle

*Hadit! Whose hiding is Nu, my living Soul! Thy secret
ardours are kissed by Nuit! Thou art Heru, Libra, the
Ordeals and Signs of the Heavens in Thy Twelvefold Glory!*

As the Moon reaches 0 degrees of Scorpio, move
anti-clockwise to face North. Stand with feet
together and raise your arms straight up into a V
(Sign of Typhon), and say

*By the Powers of the Lady of the House of Death and
Transformation, I transform!*

Burn the Confession. Preserve the ash.

3. Moon 15 degrees Scorpio

To be performed in the last hour before
the Moon reaches 15 degrees Scorpio.

Face North, and say

*I follow the Moon in the Burning Way through the
House of Death!*

Light candle

May thy light sanctify the darkness.
I offer this incense to the Underworld – blessed be thou,
creature of Earth and Fire: be thou a grateful perfume that is
acceptable to the Time.

Light incense (Myrrh)

Stand with feet together and raise your arms
straight up into a V (Sign of Typhon), and say
I invoke the Presence of Tahuti in the Palace of the Greater
Feast, and the Mother Virgin who unites and divides all
things in the Eternal Mystery of Time! Thelema! The Word
of the Law!

Take ash from the burned Confession and mark
your breast with three dots in a downward pointing
triangle, and below them, an X cross. Say

I am marked with the emblems of Death. All my success is
as a dying candle flame. With this breath

blow out candle

– to the mercy of Infinite Space and the Infinite Life thereof, I
commend my spirit and my soul.

4. Moon in Sagittarius

To be performed when the Moon is between 3 and 9 degrees of Sagittarius.

Face West. Say

I follow the Moon into the Wilderness between Worlds. I offer this incense in sacrifice to the Holy Pilgrim – blessed be thou, creature of Earth and Fire: be thou a grateful perfume that is acceptable to the Time.

Light incense (any blended perfume)

I invoke the Presence of the Winged Light! Thou art the drunkenness of pure heart! Thou art the Secret Star! Thou Desert Moon, Thou Concubine, Thou Silver Healer, I invoke Thee!

Stand with feet closely together and cross your arms on your breast (Sign of Osiris Risen), and say

By the Power of the Arrow shot swift and secure towards Heaven I live!
Aum! Such are the words.

5. Moon in Capricorn

To be performed when the Moon is between 3 and 9 degrees of Capricorn.

Face South, stand with your feet apart, arms upraised and curving forwards (Sign of Isis in Welcome), and say

*By the Power of the Glory of the Light of Heaven, I Am!
I am come with the Moon to the place of the Phoenix.
Blessed be Thy Fire!*

Light candle

*I offer this incense in sacrifice to the Company of Heaven!
Blessed be thou, creature of Earth and Fire: be thou a
grateful perfume that is acceptable to the Time.*

Light incense (Frankincense)
*I invoke the Living truth in the House of the Blessed Goat!
The Begetter and the Manifester unto the Light and of the
Light! The Grace of the Worlds!*

Contemplate the candle flame as your own spark of existence for a moment. Then snuff out the flame with the right hand and with the same fingers make an equal-armed cross over the breastbone, saying

I transfer the Living Light to my heart.
Within me is the Flame of every Star! The Shower of the
Life of Earth! Strong, and the Immortal Fire! Life in the
Eternal Now of Time! There is no god that is
not part of me.
I go forth with the light of Heaven and by the Power of Love
to do my Will upon the Earth.
So mote it be.
Amen.

4. 418 IN PRACTICE (III)

Three months of the Lunar 418 will extend from Summer through to the Autumn Equinox, when the Sun enters the 418 Quaternary. Some preparations should be made: a Pantacle with a hollow recess in the reverse, and a Wand thin enough to be broken are required for this journey, and the other two Elemental Weapons, incenses, pen and paper, water, and some beeswax. The Lunar 418 should be observed up to the Sun-Capricorn Ritual.

SUN-LIBRA

TO BE PERFORMED IN THE HOUR OF DAWN WHEN THE SUN IS BETWEEN 0 AND 3 DEGREES OF LIBRA.

Face East

This is the Time of Judgement, when the Sun is in the House of Hadit. I open this Temple of the Stars to wake the Keeper of the Balance and the Sword of Truth.

Light incense (jasmine)

Blessed be Thou, creature of Earth and Fire, may Thy perfume sanctify my way.

Take up the Wand and hold it vertically at chest level.

I am he/she who has borne the ordeals of Love and walked the Lunar Path of Judgement and Transformation under the night-stars.
In the Name of the Master of Life, Whose Numbers and Words are 4, 6, 3, 8, A, B, K, 2, 4, A:

With the Wand, make the sign of a Calvary Cross.

For the Honour of the Mother Virgin Who unites and divides Heaven and Earth, Whose Numbers and Words are L, G, M, O, R, 3, Y, X:

With the Wand, make the sign of an X Cross over the Calvary Cross..

In the Presence of the Eternal Now, Whose Numbers and Words are 24, 89, R, P, S, T, O, V, A, L:

With the Wand, make the sign of an Equal-armed Cross over the X and the Calvary Crosses.

Here:

With the Wand, encircle the three Crosses.

It is my Will to enter the Mystery of the Path Between Worlds.

Replace the Wand on the Altar.

By my Sword I swear to endure through the Ritual to come.
By my Wand I swear to endure through the Ritual to come.
By my Cup I swear to endure through the Ritual to come. By
my Pantacle I swear to endure through the Ritual to come.
The Scale of Judgement is prepared. That which serves
Heaven and has a place in the future will be preserved. That
which is to die will die.

I call ZUBENELCHEMALE, ZUBENELHAKRABI,
ZUBENELGUBI, ZUBENELGENUBI, to bear witness:
aid me in this Work!

Write the Word ABRAHADABRA on a slip of
paper.

In the Name of Life, Time, Now, and by the power of the
secret Word – let the rituals be rightly performed with joy and
beauty!
So mote it be.
Amen.

SUN-SCORPIO

To be performed in the hour of midnight
when the Sun is between 0 and 3 degrees
of Scorpio.

Face North.

*This is the Time of Ending, when the Sun is in the House
of Death. I open this Temple of the Stars to wake the Keeper
of the Doorway Between Worlds.*

Light incense (myrrh)

I sacrifice this perfume to the Company of Heaven.

Take up the Wand and hold it vertically at chest level.

*I am he/she who has borne the ordeals of Love and walked
the Lunar Path of Judgement and Transformation under the
night-stars.
In the Name of the Master of Life, Whose Numbers and
Words are 4, 6, 3, 8, A, B, K, 2, 4, A:*

With the Wand, make the sign of a Calvary Cross.

*For the Honour of the Mother Virgin Who unites and divides
Heaven and Earth, Whose Numbers and Words are L, G,
M, O, R, 3, Y, X:*

With the Wand, make the sign of an X Cross over the Calvary Cross..

In the Presence of the Eternal Now, Whose Numbers and Words are 24, 89, R, P, S, T, O, V, A, L:

With the Wand, make the sign of an Equal-armed Cross over the X and the Calvary Crosses.

Here:

With the Wand, encircle the three Crosses.

I have come from the House of Judgement with the Secret Word. It is my Will to mediate the Darkness at the Crossroads.

Replace the Wand on the Altar.

Hear me, Tahuti! Bless me as I enter the House of Death. I call GRAFFIAS, LESATH, DSCHUBBA, ALNIYAT, ANTARES, WEI, SARGAS, SHAULA, to bear witness – there is no grace, there is no guilt. Love is the Law: do what Thou wilt.
The ending of the words is the Word (silently)
ABRAHADABRA.

Burn the slip of paper. Put the ashes with the Lunar Confessions ash.

It is finished.

SUN-SAGITTARIUS

To be performed in the hour of sunset
when the Sun is between 0 and 3 degrees
of Sagittarius.

Face West.

*This is the Time of Dreaming, when the Sun is the House
of the Arrow. I open this Temple of the Stars to wake the
Keeper of the Lamp and the God that is Hereafter.*

Light incense (any desirable blend, with cedar)

*Blessed be Thou, creature of Earth and Fire, may Thy
perfume sanctify my way through the Darkness.*

Take up the Wand and hold it vertically at chest
level.

*I am he/she who has borne the ordeals of Love and walked
the Lunar Path of Judgement and Transformation under the
night-stars.
In the Name of the Master of Life, Whose Numbers and
Words are 4, 6, 3, 8, A, B, K, 2, 4, A:*

With the Wand, make the sign of a Calvary Cross.

*For the Honour of the Mother Virgin Who unites and divides
Heaven and Earth, Whose Numbers and Words are L, G,*

M, O, R, 3, Y, X:

With the Wand, make the sign of an X Cross over the Calvary Cross..

In the Presence of the Eternal Now, Whose Numbers and Words are 24, 89, R, P, S, T, O, V, A, L:

With the Wand, make the sign of an Equal-armed Cross over the X and the Calvary Crosses.

Here:

With the Wand, encircle the three Crosses.

I have followed the Solar Path from the House of Death to this Mystery of the Word in the Secret House of the Healer.

Replace the Wand on the Altar.

It is my Will to transmute the division that exists between Heaven and Earth. I invoke the Master of the Company of Heaven! By my Sword I serve Thy Truth! By my Wand I serve Thy Love! By my Cup I accept Thy Will! – that my Pantacle may be consecrated as a Temple of Earth and Heaven united.
I call ALBALDAH, NUNKI, KAUS MERIDIONALIS, ALNASR, ASCELLA, KAUS AUSTRALIS to bear witness – there is no dread hereafter.

Raise the Cup.

I accept. Not my Will but Thy Will be done.

Drink the water and replace the empty Cup. Take
up the Wand and break it in two.

*I break the Arrow of my Will. In the darkness my eyes and
my ears are closed by illusion. Before me stands the Word
(silently) ABRAHADABRA: and I wait for the Dawn.*

SUN-CAPRICORN

To be performed in the first midday hour
after the Sun has entered Capricorn.

Face South.

*Now is the Time when the Sun has entered the House of the
Blessed Goat. I open this Temple of the Stars to awaken no
God, for the Living Light is continuous in the dark before the
Dawn.*

Light incense (frankincense and rose)

May this incense be blessed and consecrated for love's sake.

Take up the Cup and hold it at chest level.

*I am he/she who has borne the ordeals of Love upon the
Lunar Path, I have been judged and I have lain in the Vault
and been no more.
In the Name of the Master of Life, Whose Numbers and
Words are 4, 6, 3, 8, A, B, K, 2, 4, A:*

With the Cup, make the sign of a Calvary Cross.

*For the Honour of the Mother Virgin Who unites and divides
Heaven and Earth, Whose Numbers and Words are L, G,
M, O, R, 3, Y, X:*

With the Cup, make the sign of an X Cross over the Calvary Cross.

In the Presence of the Eternal Now, Whose Numbers and Words are 24, 89, R, P, S, T, O, V, A, L:

With the Cup, make the sign of an Equal-armed Cross over the X and the Calvary Crosses.

Here:

With the Cup, encircle the three Crosses.

I have come from darkness to this Place of Certainty. I have broken the Wand of my Will, that it may become a Chalice of the Heart Aflame.

Replace the Cup on the Altar.

I call AL GIEDI, DABIH, NASHIRA, DENEB AL GIEDI, YEN, to bear witness and aid me in this Work, that a new Earth may be created and sealed with the promise of the Phoenix.

Place ashes in the Pantacle and seal with beeswax. Take the Pantacle to the West and raise it.

May the Powers and Spirits of Water sanctify this Pantacle of Earth!

Take the Pantacle to the North and raise it.

May the Powers and Spirits of Earth consecrate this Pantacle of Earth!

Take the Pantacle to the East and raise it.

May the Powers and Spirits of Air bless this Pantacle of Earth!

Take the Pantacle to the South and raise it.

May the Powers and Spirits of Fire purify this Pantacle of Earth!

Place the Pantacle between your feet.

I stand in the Place of Truth, with the Sight in the feet, Strong, and the Immortal Fire!

Place the Pantacle on the Altar.

I am risen in the House of the Blessed Goat, who carries the returning Light between his horns. Within me is Life in the Eternal Now of Time! Within me is the Grace of the Worlds, Who hates that evil should be wrought upon the Earth! Within me is the Flame that burns in the core of every Star and in the hearts of all! There is no Law beyond Do what Thou Wilt: there is no bond that can unite the divided but Love: Love is the Law, Love under Will: (silently) ABRAHADABRA!

Let the rituals be rightly performed with joy and beauty, ever unto Thee!
Aum:Ha.

5. 418 IN PRACTICE (iv)

For the Lunar 418 periods that occur while the Sun is in this quadrant, there is a set of rituals called "Observations" which serve to maintain the link with the Moon's progress through the Signs. The ritual timings are left to the discretion of the operator.

OBSERVATION OF MOON IN LIBRA

Face East

Thou art the Living Light (above head)
The Virgin (right shoulder)
and the Mother (left shoulder)
The Brilliance of the One Eternal Spirit (solar plexus)
Amen.

Give the Sign of Osiris Slain

By the Power of the Balance, I will Be!
Hadit! bid me within thine House to dwell.
In the Name of the Master of Life, for the Unity that divides
all things, at the ever-forming Now,
and ever unto Thee, Nuit!
Amen.

OBSERVATION OF MOON IN SCORPIO

Face North

Thou art the Living Light (above head)
The Virgin (right shoulder)
and the Mother (left shoulder)
The Brilliance of the One Eternal Spirit (solar plexus)
Amen.

Give the Sign of Typhon

By the power of the Lady of the House of Death and
Transformation, I transform!
I am alone in the House of Tahuti.
In the Name of the Master of Life, for the Unity that divides
all things, at the ever-forming Now,
and ever unto Thee, Nuit!
Amen.

OBSERVATION OF MOON IN
SAGITTARIUS

Face West

Thou art the Living Light (above head)
The Virgin (right shoulder)
and the Mother (left shoulder)
The Brilliance of the One Eternal Spirit (solar plexus)
Amen.
Give the Sign of Osiris Risen

By the Power of the Arrow shot swift and secure towards
Heaven, I live!
I walk in darkness with the Ashes of the Word.
In the Name of the Master of Life, for the Unity that divides
all things, at the ever-forming Now,
and ever unto Thee, Nuit!
Amen.

OBSERVATION OF MOON
IN CAPRICORN

Face South
Thou art the Living Light (above head)
The Virgin (right shoulder)
and the Mother (left shoulder)
The Brilliance of the One Eternal Spirit (solar plexus)
Amen.

Give the Sign of Isis In Welcome

By the Power of the Glory of the Light of Heaven, I am!
Within me is the Flame of the Life of All, in the Eternal
Now of Time!
In the Name of the Master of Life, for the Unity that divides
all things, at the ever-forming Now,
and ever unto Thee, Nuit!
Amen.

CLOSING REMARKS

In the early days EQ research was done by a functioning magical group with a permanent secret Temple, and the Sun-Venus event was often used for timing initiation rituals for new members. In the intervening decades the social stigma attached to occult studies has all but vanished, and the "oaths of dreadful secrecy" have perhaps less to do with survival in an unfriendly environment than formerly was the case; yet initiation continues to exist as a condition recognised by others who are similarly initiated. The word comes from the same root as "initial" and means taking the first step; it indicates a level of experience with magic that has moulded the intellect rather than been shaped by it. Initiation does not remove or add information, it rearranges what is there. Performing the rituals in this book will not make anyone a member of any organisation, nor confer any degree or rank – but will expand the boundaries of anyone's occult intelligence and facilitate the integration of personal magical parameters with those of the Cosmos.

Printed in the USA
CPSIA information can be obtained
at www.ICGtesting.com
LVHW021040240823
756145LV00008B/198/J

9 781914 166020